THE SKIN I AM IN

ALYCIA R. WRIGHT

WORKBOOK PRESS LLC
187 E Warm Springs Rd,
Suite B285, Las Vegas, NV 89119, USA

Website: https://workbookpress.com/
Hotline: 1-888-818-4856
Email: admin@workbookpress.com

Ordering Information:
Quantity sales. Special discounts are available on quantity purchases by corporations, associations, and others.
For details, contact the publisher at the address above.

ISBN-13:   978-1-952754-70-8 (Paperback Version)
              978-1-952754-80-7 (Digital Version)

REV. DATE: 20/10/2020

This book is dedicated to all the children who "were taught" there was something wrong with them. The lesson internalized--was a result of how the world responded to them.

Although this story eludes to color as a deference, there are many ways a child might be influenced and stigmatized...race, gender and handicap are a few. Let's build more healthy communities and rear more healthy adults by way of teaching acceptance and tolerance of the differences in our communities.

As I walked by a group of kids in my neighborhood,
I heard a whisper, then a giggle;
it couldn't have been something good.

All the kids alike in this one group
of fair and lighter skin.
They blurted things quite mean to me,
about the skin I'm in.

One little girl had yellow hair.
I saw a boy with eyes sky blue.
Another kid had big, brown freckles
and he seemed to me quite rude.

There was a kid with dirty jeans.
A boy with one short arm.
They all in common jeered at me;
with statements not so warm.

I saw differences from short to tall.
They had assorted eyes and hair.
They found me as an alien;
I knew it by their glare.

They referred to me as "Black Kid,"
and "nappy-head" they jeered!
An alliance of their color
was dismal and quite clear.

On Tuesday I had helped that girl,
with the curly, yellow hair.
She had tripped and fell
then skinned her knee,
on the back hall stair.

We never spoke a word after
that day. Dared neither she nor I.
Yet as I helped to gather books,
she whispered, "Thanks—goodbye."

The boy with blue eyes smiled at me,
while in the grocery store.
We both mused through the magazines,
as our moms perused the floors.

I played secretly with Tommy;
on just the other day.
The kid with big, brown freckles,
so why the sneer today?

I wondered if the others knew
that early in the week
Mike and I sat in the grocery store,
an alliance we did peak.

How could they point—harass me?
I never understood.
I never was a mean kid,
actually, I was quite good.

I got good grades and did my chores
"unto others did I do,"
The Golden Rule in Kindergarten;
what "you want done unto you."

They would play and talk when we were alone;
but in public formed a band.
On opposite teams, formed akin,
chosen by the color of the skin we were in.

Did Suzy with the curly hair
tell of her trip down back hall stairs?
Did Lance delight more in the jeers,
than our secret playful affair?

I wonder if their parents
were just as mean as they?
If I knocked upon their door,
would they shout "Go away?"

Why is it that in public
we choose to eat in a troop,
guided by color code and gender
and even ethnic group?

If the United States is equal
in opportunity,
then why outright distinction
based on race and color or creed?

A kid is a kid. A man is a man.
Your mom and my mom too . . .
In common help with homework,
and feel sad if we are blue.

If I had one wish, it would not be
for money or great things.
I would not ask for fancy cars.
No fine toys, diamond rings, or bling.

I would wish for a world with people
who were treated all the same.
No matter what distinction
except what we are named.

I would erase the fear surrounding
our differences, indeed!
Allow our positive experiences
to be the root of what is perceived.

The character of a person
would be earned along the way.
Not decided by a myth,
but by what one has done today.

CPSIA information can be obtained
at www.ICGtesting.com
Printed in the USA
BVHW091714250621
610384BV00017B/1358

9 781952 754708